INVESTMENT LAW

Essential Legal Terms Explained You Need To Know About Law On Investment!

DR. PETER JOHNSON

Copyright © 2019

All rights reserved.

ISBN: 9781798524558

TEXT COPYRIGHT © [DR. PETER JOHNSON]

all rights reserved. No part of this guide may be reproduced in any form without permission in writing from the publisher except in the case of brief quotations embodied in critical articles or reviews.

Legal & disclaimer

The information contained in this book and its contents is not designed to replace or take the place of any form of medical or professional advice; and is not meant to replace the need for independent medical, financial, legal or other professional advice or services, as may be required. The content and information in this book have been provided for educational and entertainment purposes only.

The content and information contained in this book have been compiled from sources deemed reliable, and it is accurate to the best of the author's knowledge, information, and belief. However, the author cannot guarantee its accuracy and validity and cannot be held liable for any errors and/or omissions. Further, changes are periodically made to this book as and when needed. Where appropriate and/or necessary, you must consult a professional (including but not limited to your doctor, attorney, financial advisor or such other professional advisor) before using any of the suggested remedies, techniques, or information in this book.

Upon using the contents and information contained in this book, you agree to hold harmless the author from and against any damages, costs, and expenses, including any legal fees potentially resulting from the application of any of the information provided by this book. This disclaimer applies to any loss, damages or injury caused by the use and application, whether directly or indirectly, of any advice or information presented, whether for breach of contract, tort, negligence, personal injury, criminal intent, or under any other cause of action.

You agree to accept all risks of using the information presented inside this book.

You agree that by continuing to read this book, where appropriate and/or necessary, you shall consult a professional (including but not limited to your doctor, attorney, or financial advisor or such other advisor as needed) before using any of the suggested remedies, techniques, or information in this book.

Table of Contents

Introduction 8

Explanation Of Terms 9

Policies On Business Investment 11

Banned Business Lines 12

Conditional Business Lines 13

Guarantees Relating To Capital And Assets 14

Opening Markets And Investments Related To Trade 15

Protection Of Intellectual Property Rights 16

Assurance Of Business Investment 17

Assurance Of Business Investment Upon Changes Of Laws .. 18

Assurance Of Transfer Of Foreign Investors' Assets To Abroad 19

Application Of Uniform Prices, Fees And Charges 20

Right To Autonomy In Investment - Business 21

Right To Access And Use Investment Resources 22

Right To Import And Export, To Conduct Marketing And Advertise, To Process And Re-Process Goods Relevant To Investment Activities 23

Right To Purchase Foreign Currencies 24

Right To Assign Or Adjust Capital Or Investment Project 25

Mortgage Of Land Use Rights And Of Assets Attached To Land 26

Other Rights Of Investors 27

Obligations Of Investors 28

Forms Of Investment 29

Investment In Establishment Of A Business Organization 29

Making Investment By Contributing Capital, Buying Shares, Or Buying Capital Contributions Of Business Organizations . 30

Methods And Conditions For Making Capital Contributions To Business Organizations, Buying Shares Or Capital Contributions Of Business Organizations 31

Investment In Accordance With Contract 32

Investment In Business Development 33

Capital Contribution, Purchase Of Shareholding, Merger And Acquisition 34

Indirect Investment 35

Incentive Investment Sectors 36

Sectors In Which Investment Is Conditional 37

Sectors In Which Investment Is Prohibited 38

Geographical Areas Of Investment Incentives 39

Investment Incentives 40

Applicable Entities And Conditions For Investment Incentives 40

Tax Incentives 41

Carrying Forward Losses 42

Depreciation Of Fixed Assets 43

Incentives Applicable To Investors Who Invest In Industrial Zones, Export Processing Zones, High-Tech Zones, And Economic Zones 44

Procedures For Implementation Of Investment Incentives 45

Circumstances In Which Incentives May Be Extended 46

Contents Of Certificate Of Investment Registration 47

Temporary Postponement Of Projects; Revocation Of Investment Certificates 48

Codes Of Investment Project 49

Termination Of Operation Of Investment Projects 50

Offshore Investment 51

Forms Of Outward Investment 52

Conditions For Offshore Investment 53

Sources Of Capital For Outward Investment 54

Rights Of Offshore Investors 55

Obligations Of Offshore Investors 56

Contents Of Certificate Of Registration Of Outward Investment 57

Termination Of An Outward Investment Project 58

Use Of Profit For Overseas Investment 59

National Investment Information System 60

Review, Assessment Of Implementation Of Regulations On Business Lines Subject To Conditions 61

Procedures For Execution Of Investment Projects 62

Performance Security 63

Procedures For Adjusting A Project In Case Of Corporate Division, Acquisition, Consolidation, Or Conversion 64

Procedures For Investment Through Capital Contribution, Purchase Of Shares/Stakes By Foreign Investors 65

Operation Of Investors Executing Investment Projects In Industrial Parks, Export-Processing Zones, Economic Zones, And Hi-Tech Zones 66

Operation Of Investors Executing Investment Projects And Operating Infrastructure Of Industrial Parks, Export-Processing Zones, Economic Zones, And Hi-Tech Zones 67

Sending Reports 68

Responsibilities For Project Formulation, Making Investment Decisions And Evaluating Investments 69

Selection Of Investor For Project Where A Number Of Investors Show Interest 70

Preparation Of Construction Sites 71

Procedures For Implementing Investment Projects Involving Mining And Use Of Natural Resources And Minerals 72

Implementation Of Investment Projects Involving Construction 73

Conclusion 74

Check Out Other Books 75

Introduction

Thank you and congratulate you for downloading the book *"INVESTMENT: Essential Legal Terms Explained You Need To Know About Law On Investment"*

With a clear, concise, and engaging writing style, Dr. Peter Johnson will help you with a practical understanding of investment law topics about business investment, investments related to trade, rights of investors, obligations of investors, forms of investment, direct investment, indirect investment, investment incentives, offshore investment; provide you a road map to navigating investment rules and help you build a foundation for understanding the overall picture and much much more. This book delivers extensive coverage of every aspect of the law and details the duties a paralegal is expected to perform when working within investment law. High-level, comprehensive coverage is combined with cutting-edge developments and foundational concepts.

As the author of the book, I promise this book will be an invaluable source of legal reference for professionals, international lawyers, law students, business professionals and anyone else who want to improve their use of legal terminology, succinct clarification of legal terms and have a better understanding of investment law. All legal terms and phrases are well written and explained clearly in plain English.

Thank you again for purchasing this book, and I hope you enjoy it.

Let's get started!

EXPLANATION OF TERMS

1. *Investment* means the use of capital in the form of tangible or intangible assets for the purposes of forming assets by investors to carry out investment activities.

2. *Direct investment* means a form of investment whereby the investor invests its invested capital and participates in the management of the investment activity.

3. *Indirect investment* means a form of investment through the purchase of shares, share certificates, bonds, other valuable papers or investment through a securities investment fund and through other intermediary financial institutions and whereby the investor does not participate directly in the management of the investment activity.

4. *Investor* means any organization or individual carrying out investment activities.

5. *Investment activity* means activities of investors throughout the investment process, comprising the stages of investment preparation, performance and management of the investment project.

6. *Register office* means the regulatory body competent to issue, adjust, and revoke Certificates of investment registration.

7. *Investment project* means a collection of proposal to make midterm or long-term capital investment in business in a particular administrative division over a certain period of time.

8. *Expansion project* means a project to make investment to expand the scale, improve the capacity, apply new technologies, reduce pollution or improve the environment.

9. *New investment project* means a project that is executed for the first time or a project independent from any other running project.

10. *Business investment* means an investor's investing capital to do business by establishing a business organization; making capital contribution, buying shares or capital contributions to a business organization; making investments in the form of contracts or execution of investment projects.

11. *Certificate of investment registration* means a paper or electronic document bearing registered information about the investment project of the investor.

12. *National investment database* means a system of professional information meant for monitoring, assessment, and analysis of investments nationwide in order to serve state management tasks and support for investors' investment making process.

13. *Public-Private Partnership contract (hereinafter referred to as PPP contract)* means a contract between a competent authority and an investor or project management enterprise to execute an investment project as prescribed in Article 27 of the Law on Investment.

14. *Business cooperation contract* means a contract between investors for business cooperation and distribution of profits, products without establishment of a new business organization.

15. *Export-processing zone* means an industrial park specialized in manufacturing of exported products or provision of services for manufacturing of exported products and export.

16. *Industrial park* means an area with a defined geographical boundary specialized in industrial production and provision of services for industrial production.

17. *Economic zone* means an area with a defined geographical boundary which consists of multiple sectors and is meant to attract investments, develop socio-economic, and protect national defense and security.

18. *Business organization* include companies, cooperatives, cooperative associations, and other organizations that make business investments.

19. *Foreign-invested business organization* means a business whose members or shareholders are foreign investors.

20. *Capital* means money and other assets used invested in business.

POLICIES ON BUSINESS INVESTMENT

1. Investors are entitled to make investments in the business lines that are not banned in the Law on Investment.

2. Investors may decide their business investments on their own; may access and make use of loan capital, assistance funds, land, and other resources as prescribed by law.

3. The ownership of assets, capital, income, another the lawful rights and interests of investors are recognized and protected by the State.

4. The State shall treat investors equitably; introduce policies to encourage and enable investors to make business investment and to ensure sustainable development of economic sectors.

5. The State shall encourage and shall have a policy of incentives applicable to investment in investment incentive sectors and geographical areas.

BANNED BUSINESS LINES

The investments in the activities below are banned:

a) Trade in the narcotic substances;

n) Trade in the chemicals and minerals;

c) Trade in specimens of wild flora and fauna;

d) Prostitution;

dd) Human trafficking; trade in human tissues and body parts;

e) Business pertaining to human cloning.

CONDITIONAL BUSINESS LINES

Conditional business lines are the business lines in which the investment must satisfy certain conditions for reasons of national defense and security, social order and security, social ethics, or public health.

GUARANTEES RELATING TO CAPITAL AND ASSETS

1. Lawful assets and invested capital of investors shall not be nationalized or confiscated by administrative measures.

2. Where an asset is bought or commandeered by the State of reasons of national defense and security, national interests, state of emergency, prevention or recovery of natural disaster, the investor shall be reimbursed or compensated in accordance with regulations of law on property commandeering and relevant regulations of law.

Payment of compensation or damages must ensure the lawful interests of investors and be made on the basis of non-discrimination between investors.

3. Any compensation or damages payable to foreign investors as stipulated in clause 2 of this article shall be made in a freely convertible currency and shall be permitted to be remitted abroad.

4. Procedures and conditions for compulsory acquisition and requisition [shall be implemented] in accordance with law.

OPENING MARKETS AND INVESTMENTS RELATED TO TRADE

In order to comply with the provisions of international treaties of which the home country is a member, the State guarantees to implement the following provisions in respect of foreign investors:

1. To open the investment market in compliance with the committed schedule;

2. Not to compel investors to undertake the following requirements:

(a) To give priority to the purchase or use of domestic goods or services; or to purchase compulsorily goods from a specific domestic manufacturer or services from a specific domestic service provider;

(b) To export goods or services at a fixed percentage; to restrict the quantity, value or type of goods or services which may be exported or of goods which may be manufactured domestically or services which may be provided domestically;

(c) To import goods at the same quantity and value as goods exported, or to self-balance compulsorily foreign currency from sources obtained from exported goods in order to satisfy their import requirements;

(d) To achieve certain localization ratios during manufacture of goods;

(dd) To achieve a stipulated level or value in their research and development activities in the home country;

(e) To supply goods or provide services in a particular location whether in the home country or abroad;

(g) To establish its head office in a particular location.

PROTECTION OF INTELLECTUAL PROPERTY RIGHTS

The State shall protect intellectual property rights during investment activities; and shall ensure the legitimate rights of investors in technology transfer in accordance with the laws on intellectual property and other provisions of the relevant laws.

ASSURANCE OF BUSINESS INVESTMENT

Investors are not required by the State to satisfy the following requirements:

a) Give priority to buying, using domestic goods/services; or only buy, use goods/services provided by local producers/service providers;

b) Achieve a certain export target; restrict the quantity, value, types of goods/services that are exported or produced/provided in the home country;

c) Import a quantity/value of goods that is equivalent to the quantity/value of goods exported; or balance foreign currencies earned from export to meet import demands;

d) Reach a certain rate of import substitution;

dd) Reach a certain level/value of domestic research and development;

e) Provide goods/service at a particular location in the home country or overseas;

g) Have the headquarter situated at a location requested by a competent authority.

ASSURANCE OF BUSINESS INVESTMENT UPON CHANGES OF LAWS

1. Where a new law that provides more favorable investment incentives that those currently enjoyed by investor is promulgated, investors shall enjoy the new incentives for the remaining period of the incentive enjoyment of the project.

2. Where a new law that provides less favorable investment incentives that those currently enjoyed by investor is promulgated, investors shall keep enjoying the current incentives for the remaining period of the incentive enjoyment of the project.

ASSURANCE OF TRANSFER OF FOREIGN INVESTORS' ASSETS TO ABROAD

After all financial obligations to the government are fulfilled, foreign investors are permitted to transfer the following assets to abroad:

1. Capital and liquidations;

2. Income from business investment;

3. Money and other assets under the lawful ownership of the investors.

APPLICATION OF UNIFORM PRICES, FEES AND CHARGES

During the process of an investment activity, the investor shall be entitled to uniform application of price rates for goods and fees and charges for services which are controlled by the State.

RIGHT TO AUTONOMY IN INVESTMENT - BUSINESS

Investors shall have the following rights:

1. To select the sector in which to make an investment, the form of investment, the method of raising capital, the geographical location and scale of the investment; an investment partner and the duration of operation of the project.

2. To register business in one or more industries and trades, to establish enterprises in accordance with law and to make its own decisions concerning its registered investment - business activities.

RIGHT TO ACCESS AND USE INVESTMENT RESOURCES

Investors shall have the following rights:

1. Equality in access to and use of sources of credit capital and aid funds, and in use of land and natural resources in accordance with law.

2. To lease or purchase equipment and machinery either domestically or overseas in order to carry out an investment project.

3. To recruit domestic employees; to recruit foreign employees to fulfil management tasks, to provide technical labour and to provide expertise in accordance with production and business requirements.

RIGHT TO IMPORT AND EXPORT, TO CONDUCT MARKETING AND ADVERTISE, TO PROCESS AND RE-PROCESS GOODS RELEVANT TO INVESTMENT ACTIVITIES

Investors shall have the following rights:

1. To import directly or to import by way of authorized dealers; equipment, machinery, raw materials, supplies and goods for investment activities; and to export directly or to export by way of authorized dealers and to sell its products.

2. To advertise and market its products and services and to enter into advertising contracts directly with organizations which are authorized to publish advertisements.

3. To undertake activities being processing or reprocessing of products; to place orders for processing or reprocessing of goods domestically, or to place orders for processing of goods overseas in accordance with the commercial law.

RIGHT TO PURCHASE FOREIGN CURRENCIES

1. Investors shall be permitted to purchase foreign currencies from credit institutions authorized to conduct foreign currency business in order to meet the demand of their current transactions, capital transactions and other transactions in accordance with the provisions of the law on foreign exchange control.

2. The Government shall guarantee or assist the foreign currency balance of a number of important projects in the sectors of energy, construction of traffic infrastructure facilities and waste treatment.

RIGHT TO ASSIGN OR ADJUST CAPITAL OR INVESTMENT PROJECT

1. Investors shall have the right to assign or adjust capital or an investment project. Where profits arise from an assignment, the assignor must pay income tax in accordance with law.

2. The Government shall provide conditions for assignment or adjustment of capital or investment projects in cases where such conditions are required.

MORTGAGE OF LAND USE RIGHTS AND OF ASSETS ATTACHED TO LAND

Investors having investment projects shall be permitted to mortgage land use rights and assets attached to land in order to borrow capital for implementation of projects in accordance with law.

OTHER RIGHTS OF INVESTORS

Investors shall have the following rights:

1. To receive investment incentives in accordance with provisions of the relevant laws.

2. To have access to and use public services on the principle of non-discrimination.

3. To have access to legal instruments and policies relating to investment; to data on the national economy, to data about each economic sector and to other relevant information about investment activities; and to contribute its opinions on laws and policies relating to investment.

4. To lodge complaints, to make denunciations or to institute legal proceedings relating to breaches of the law by organizations and individuals in accordance with law.

5. To exercise other rights in accordance with law.

OBLIGATIONS OF INVESTORS

Investors shall have the following obligations:

1. To comply with the provisions of the laws on investment procedures; to carry out investment activities correctly in accordance with the registered investment contents [and/or] the provisions of the investment certificate.

The investor shall be responsible for the accuracy and truthfulness of the contents of investment registration and of the investment project file and the lawfulness of documents on certification.

2. To discharge fully financial obligations in accordance with law.

3. To carry out the provisions of the laws on accounting, auditing and statistics.

4. To perform obligations in accordance with the law on insurance, on labour;

5. To respect and create favourable conditions for employees to establish or participate in political organizations and socio-political organizations.

6. To implement the provisions of the law on protection of the environment.

7. To perform other obligations in accordance with law.

FORMS OF INVESTMENT

INVESTMENT IN ESTABLISHMENT OF A BUSINESS ORGANIZATION

1. Investors may establish business organizations in accordance with law. Before establishing a business organization, the foreign investor must have an investment project and apply for a Certificate of investment registration following the procedures of the Law.

2. Every foreign investor shall execute the investment project via a business organization established.

3. Foreign investors may own an indefinite amount of charter capital invested in business organizations.

MAKING INVESTMENT BY CONTRIBUTING CAPITAL, BUYING SHARES, OR BUYING CAPITAL CONTRIBUTIONS OF BUSINESS ORGANIZATIONS

1. Investors are entitled to contribute capital, buy shares, or buy capital contributions of business organizations.

2. Foreign investors making investment by contributing capital, buying shares, buying capital contribution of business organizations shall comply with regulations of the Law on Investment.

METHODS AND CONDITIONS FOR MAKING CAPITAL CONTRIBUTIONS TO BUSINESS ORGANIZATIONS, BUYING SHARES OR CAPITAL CONTRIBUTIONS OF BUSINESS ORGANIZATIONS

1. Foreign investors may contribute capital to business organizations in the following manners:

a) Buy shares of joint-stock companies through IPOs or additional issuance;

b) Contribute capitals to limited liability companies and partnerships;

2. Foreign investors shall buy shares or capital contributions of business organization in the following manners:

a) Buy shares of joint-stock companies from the companies or their shareholders;

b) Buy capital contributions to limited liability companies by their members and become members of limited liability companies;

c) Buy capital contributions to partnerships by partners and become partners;

INVESTMENT IN ACCORDANCE WITH CONTRACT

1. Investors shall be permitted to sign a BCC contract in order to co-operate in production and to share profits or to share products and other forms of business co-operation.

The contract shall set out the co-operating parties; the contents of the co-operation; the duration of business; the rights, obligations and responsibilities of each party; the co-operative relationship between the parties and the management organization as agreed by the parties.

A BCC contract in the sector of prospecting, exploration and mining of petroleum and some other natural resources and in the form of a production sharing contract shall be implemented in accordance with the provisions of the relevant laws.

2. Investors shall be permitted to sign a BOT, BTO and BT contract with the competent State body in order to implement projects for new construction, expansion, modernization and operation of infrastructure projects in the sectors of traffic, electricity production and business, water supply or drainage, waste treatment and other sectors as stipulated by the Prime Minister of the Government.

The Government shall provide regulations on investment sectors; on the conditions, order, procedures and methods of implementation of investment projects; and on the rights and obligations of the parties implementing an investment project in the contractual form of BOT, BTO and BT.

INVESTMENT IN BUSINESS DEVELOPMENT

Investors shall be permitted to invest in business development through the following forms:

1. Expanding scale, increasing output capacity and business capability.

2. Renovating technology, improving product quality and reducing environmental pollution.

CAPITAL CONTRIBUTION, PURCHASE OF SHAREHOLDING, MERGER AND ACQUISITION

1. Investors shall be permitted to contribute capital to and to purchase shareholding in companies and branches.

The ratio of capital contribution and purchase of shareholding by foreign investors in a number of sectors, industries and trades shall be regulated by the Government.

2. Investors shall be permitted to merge and to acquire companies and branches.

The conditions for merger and acquisition of companies and branches shall be regulated by the law on investment, the law on competition and other provisions of the relevant laws.

INDIRECT INVESTMENT

1. Investors shall be permitted to carry out the following forms of indirect investment:

(a) Purchase of shareholding, shares, bonds and other valuable papers;

(b) Through securities investment funds;

(c) Through other intermediary financial institutions.

2. Any investment by way of purchase or sale of shares, share certificates, bonds and other valuable papers of individuals and organizations and procedures for conducting indirect investment activities shall be implemented in accordance with the law on securities and other provisions of the relevant laws.

INCENTIVE INVESTMENT SECTORS

[shall comprise:]

1. Manufacture of new materials and production of new energy; manufacture of high-tech products; bio-technologies; information technology; mechanical manufacturing.

2. Breeding, rearing, growing and processing agricultural, forestry and aquaculture products; production of salt; creation of new plant and animal variety.

3. Use of high technology and advanced techniques; protection of the ecological environment; research, development and creation of high-technology.

4. Labour intensive industries.

5. Construction and development of infrastructure facilities and important industrial projects with a large scale.

6. Professional development of education, training, health, sports, physical education and culture.

7. Development of traditional crafts and industries.

SECTORS IN WHICH INVESTMENT IS CONDITIONAL

Sectors in which investment is subject to conditions shall comprise:

(a) Sectors impacting on national defence and security, social order and safety;

(b) Banking and finance sector;

(c) Sectors impacting on public health;

(d) Culture, information, the press and publishing;

(dd) Entertainment services;

(e) Real estate business;

(g) Survey, prospecting, exploration and mining of natural resources; the ecological environment;

(h) Development of education and training;

SECTORS IN WHICH INVESTMENT IS PROHIBITED

Investment activities shall be prohibited in the following sectors:

1. Projects which are detrimental to national defence and security, and the public interest.

2. Projects which are detrimental to historical and cultural traditions and ethics, and local fine customs.

3. Projects which harm the people's health, or which destroy natural resources and the environment.

4. Projects for the manufacture of any type of toxic chemicals or for the use of chemical agents prohibited by international treaties.

GEOGRAPHICAL AREAS OF INVESTMENT INCENTIVES

Investment shall be encouraged in the following areas:

1. Areas with difficult socio-economic conditions; areas with specially difficult socio-economic conditions.

2. Industrial zones, export processing zones, high-tech zones and economic zones.

INVESTMENT INCENTIVES

APPLICABLE ENTITIES AND CONDITIONS FOR INVESTMENT INCENTIVES

1. Investors with investment projects in the investment incentive sectors and geographical areas shall be entitled to the incentives as stipulated in the Law on Investment and other provisions of the relevant laws.

2. The investment incentives shall be applicable to new investment projects and investment projects for expansion of scale, for raising output capacity or business capacity; for renovation of technology or raising product quality, or for reducing environmental pollution.

TAX INCENTIVES

1. Investors having projects within the categories shall be entitled to preferential tax rates, the duration of entitlement to such rates and the duration of exemption from and reduction of tax in accordance with the law on tax.

2. Investors shall be entitled to tax incentives on that portion of income which is distributed to them from an activity being capital contribution or purchase of shareholding in an economic organization in accordance with the law on tax after such organization has paid in full corporate income tax.

3. Investors shall be exempt from payment of import duty on equipment, materials, means of transportation and other goods for implementation of investment projects in the home country in accordance with the Law on Export and Import Duties.

4. Income from activities of technology transfer applicable to projects entitled to investment incentives shall be exempt from income tax in accordance with the law on tax.

CARRYING FORWARD LOSSES

If an investor suffers losses after completion of tax finalization with the tax office, it shall be permitted to carry its losses forward to the following year, and the amount of such losses shall be set off against taxable income for the purposes of corporate income tax in accordance with the Law on Corporate Income Tax. The period for carrying forward losses shall not exceed five years.

DEPRECIATION OF FIXED ASSETS

Investment projects in investment incentive sectors and geographical areas and business projects with high economic efficiency shall be subject to accelerated depreciation of fixed assets; the maximum rate of depreciation shall not be more than twice the level of depreciation as stipulated by regulations on depreciation of fixed assets.

INCENTIVES APPLICABLE TO INVESTORS WHO INVEST IN INDUSTRIAL ZONES, EXPORT PROCESSING ZONES, HIGH-TECH ZONES, AND ECONOMIC ZONES

Based on the conditions for socio-economic development in each period and the principles stipulated in the Law on Investment, the Government shall provide for incentives applicable to investors investing in industrial zones, export processing zones, high-tech zones and economic zones.

PROCEDURES FOR IMPLEMENTATION OF INVESTMENT INCENTIVES

1. With respect to domestic investment projects in the category for which investment is not registered and projects in the category for which investment is registered, investors shall, on the basis of the incentives and conditions for investment incentives stipulated by law, assess themselves incentives and shall conduct procedures at the competent State body for investment incentives.

If an investor requests the certification of investment incentives, it shall conduct the procedures for investment registration in order for the State administrative body for investment to record investment incentives in the investment certificate.

2. With respect to domestic investment projects in the category for which there must be evaluation for investment and which satisfy the conditions for incentives, the State administrative body for investment shall record incentives in the investment certificate.

3. With respect to foreign invested projects which satisfy the conditions for incentives, the State administrative body for investment shall record investment incentives in the investment certificate.

CIRCUMSTANCES IN WHICH INCENTIVES MAY BE EXTENDED

Where encouragement of the development of an especially important branch, a zone or a special economic zone is required, the Government may make a submission to the National Assembly for its consideration and issuance of a resolution on investment incentives other than those stipulated in the law on investment.

CONTENTS OF CERTIFICATE OF INVESTMENT REGISTRATION

1. Code of the project.

2. Name and address of the investor.

3. Name of the project.

4. Location and area of the project.

5. Objectives and scale of the project.

6. Capital investment in the project (including the investor's capital and raised capital), capital contribution and capital raising schedule.

7. Duration of the project.

8. Project execution schedule: schedule of infrastructural development and inauguration (if any); schedule of achievements of primary targets and items; targets, duration, and operations of each stage (if the project is divided into multiple stages);

9. Investment incentives, support, and conditions (if any).

10. Conditions applied to the investor (if any).

TEMPORARY POSTPONEMENT OF PROJECTS; REVOCATION OF INVESTMENT CERTIFICATES

1. If an investor postpones temporarily an investment project, the investor must report to the State administrative body for investment for verification of any grounds for a consideration of exemption or reduction of land rent during the period for which the project is temporarily postponed.

2. With respect to investment projects which have been issued with an investment certificate, if after twelve (12) months the investor has failed to proceed with implementation of the project in accordance with the schedule undertaken without a legitimate reason, the issued investment certificate shall be revoked.

CODES OF INVESTMENT PROJECT

1. A code of an investment project is a 10-digit number automatically generated by National Foreign Investment Information System and written on the Investment Registration Certificate.

2. Each investment project has a single code which remains unchanged throughout the operation of the project and must not be given to another project. The code of an investment project expires when the investment project is shut down.

3. Competent authority shall use codes of investment projects uniformly to manage and exchange information about investment projects.

TERMINATION OF OPERATION OF INVESTMENT PROJECTS

The operation of an investment project shall be terminated in any one of the following cases:

1. Upon expiry of the duration of operation as stipulated in the investment certificate.

2. In accordance with the conditions which will result in termination as stipulated in the contract, charter of the enterprise or agreement or undertakings of investors about the project implementation schedule.

3. Where the investor decides to terminate the operation of the project.

4. The operation is terminated in accordance with the decision of the State administrative body for investment or a judgement or decision of the court or arbitration due to a breach of law.

OFFSHORE INVESTMENT

1. Investors shall be permitted to make offshore investments in accordance with the law of the investment recipient country.

2. The State shall facilitate offshore investments and shall protect the interests of investors overseas in accordance with the provisions of international treaties.

FORMS OF OUTWARD INVESTMENT

Outward investments in the following forms:

a) Establishing a business organization in accordance with the law of the host country;

b) Execute a business cooperation contract overseas;

c) Purchase part or all of charter capital of an overseas business organization to participate in the management and business investment overseas;

d) Trading in securities, valuable papers, or making investments via securities investment funds and other intermediate financial institutions overseas;

dd) Other forms of investments prescribed by law of the host country.

CONDITIONS FOR OFFSHORE INVESTMENT

1. In order to be permitted to make an offshore investment in the form of a direct investment, investors must satisfy all of the following conditions:

(a) Have an offshore investment project;

(b) Have discharged all financial obligations to the State of the home country;

(c) Have an investment certificate as issued by the State administrative body for investment.

2. Offshore investments in the form of an indirect investment must comply with the laws on banking and securities and with other provisions of the relevant laws.

3. The use of State-owned capital to make offshore investments must comply with the law on management and use of State-owned capital.

SOURCES OF CAPITAL FOR OUTWARD INVESTMENT

The investor shall invest and raise capital to make investments overseas. Conditions and procedures for taking foreign currency loans and transferring foreign currency capital must comply with regulations of law on banking, credit institutions, and foreign currency management.

RIGHTS OF OFFSHORE INVESTORS

An offshore investor shall have the following rights:

1. To remit overseas investment capital in lawful cash or other assets in order to implement an investment in accordance with the law on foreign exchange control after the competent body of the offshore country or territory has approved the investment project.

2. To be entitled to investment incentives in accordance with law.

3. To recruit domestic employees in order to send them overseas to work in the business and production establishments which the investor establishes overseas.

OBLIGATIONS OF OFFSHORE INVESTORS

An offshore investor shall have the following obligations:

1. To comply with the law of the investment recipient country.

2. To repatriate profit and other income from offshore investment activities in accordance with law.

3. To comply with the financial reporting and operational reporting regime of the investment recipient country.

4. To discharge fully financial obligations to the State.

CONTENTS OF CERTIFICATE OF REGISTRATION OF OUTWARD INVESTMENT

1. Code of the investment project.
2. Name and address of the investor.
3. Name of the investment project.
4. Objectives and location of the project.
5. Capital and capital sources; capital contribution and capital raising schedule; overseas investment schedule;
6. Rights and obligations of the investor.
7. Incentives and support (if any).

TERMINATION OF AN OUTWARD INVESTMENT PROJECT

An outward investment project shall be terminated in the following cases:

a) The investor decides to terminate the project;

b) The project duration is over;

c) The project is terminated according to the regulations of the contract or company's charter;

d) The investor transfers all of overseas capital to a foreign investor;

dd) The project is not approved by the host country after 12 months from the date of issue of the Certificate of outward investment registration, or the project is not commenced after 12 months from the day on which it is approved by a competent authority of the host country;

e) The investor fails to execute the project or is not able to execute the project according to the registered schedule after 12 months from the date of issue of the Certificate of investment registration, and does not adjust the investment schedule;

g) The investor fails to submit a written report on the operation of the project after 12 months from the day on which the annual tax declaration or an equivalent document is available as prescribed by the host country's law;

h) The overseas business organization is dissolved or goes bankrupt as prescribed by the host country's law;

i) The project is terminated under the decision or judgment of the court or arbitral tribunal.

USE OF PROFIT FOR OVERSEAS INVESTMENT

1. The investor that uses profit derived from overseas investment to increase capital, expand overseas investment shall follow procedures for adjusting the Certificate of outward investment registration and submit a report to the local State bank.

2. If profit derived from the overseas project is used for another overseas project, the investor shall follow procedures for the Certificate of outward investment registration of such project, register a capital account and monetary capital transfer schedule with the local State bank.

NATIONAL INVESTMENT INFORMATION SYSTEM

1. National Investment Information System consists of:

a) National Information System for Domestic Investment;

b) National Information System for Inward and Outward Investments.

2. Investment authorities and investors shall promptly and accurately update information on National Investment Information System.

3. Information about investment projects in National Investment Information System is considered original and lawful information.

REVIEW, ASSESSMENT OF IMPLEMENTATION OF REGULATIONS ON BUSINESS LINES SUBJECT TO CONDITIONS

1. Annually and on demand, Ministries and ministerial agencies shall review, assess the implementation of regulations on business lines subject to conditions and investment conditions under their management.

2. Review and assessment content:

a) Assess the implementation of regulations of law on to business lines subject to conditions and investment conditions under their management at the time of review, assessment;

b) Assess the impacts and effectiveness of regulations on business lines subject to conditions and investment conditions; difficulties that arise during the course of implementation;

c) Assess the socio-economic changes, technological changes, management requirements, and other conditions that affect the implementation of regulations on business lines subject to conditions and investment conditions (if any);

d) Propose amendments to regulations on business lines subject to conditions and investment conditions (if any);

3. Ministries and ministerial agencies shall send their proposals to the Ministry of Planning and Investment for consolidation and reporting to the Prime Minister.

PROCEDURES FOR EXECUTION OF INVESTMENT PROJECTS

1. During the process of execution of an investment project, the investor shall comply with regulations of law on investment, construction, land, environmental protection, employment, and relevant regulations of law.

2. With regard to an investment project executed under the Investment Registration Certificate or decision on investment guidelines, the investor shall execute it in accordance with the Investment Registration Certificate or decision on investment guidelines and relevant regulations of law.

3. The investor shall report investment activities in accordance with the Law on Investment, and relevant regulations of law; provide documents and information related to investment inspection and supervision for competent authorities as prescribed by law.

PERFORMANCE SECURITY

The investor must pay a deposit when receiving land, leasing land, or permitted to repurpose land by the State to execute the investment project, except for the following cases:

a) The investor is the successful bidder for land use right to execute the investment project and receives levied land from the State or leases land from the State and pay a lump sum rent for the entire lease term;

b) The investor is a successful bidder for an investment project using land according to regulations of law on bidding;

c) The investor receives land or lease land from the State on the basis of transfer of an investment project has paid the deposit of completely contributed capital and/or raised capital according to the schedule specified in the Investment Registration Certificate or decision on investment guidelines;

d) The investor receives land or leases land from the State to execute an investment project on the basis of receipt of land use right or property on land of another land user;

dd) The investor is a revenue-earning public service agency, a hi-tech zone development company established under a decision of a competent authority to execute investment projects that receive land or lease land from the State to develop infrastructure of industrial parks, export-processing zones, hi-tech zones, specialized areas in economic zones.

PROCEDURES FOR ADJUSTING A PROJECT IN CASE OF CORPORATE DIVISION, ACQUISITION, CONSOLIDATION, OR CONVERSION

1. A business organization established on the basis of a corporate division, acquisition, consolidation, or conversion shall inherit the investor's rights and obligations to the investment project before restructuring.

2. The investor shall decide the restructuring and settle the assets, rights and obligations to the project in accordance with regulations of law on enterprises and relevant regulations of law.

3. The investor shall submit an application for project adjustments to the investment registration authority of the administrative division in which the project is located. The application consists of:

a) A written request for permission for project adjustments;

b) Copies of the Certificate of Enterprise Registration or an equivalent document of the transferee;

c) Copies of the investor's resolution or decision on restructuring which specifies the settlement of assets, rights and obligations to the project.

PROCEDURES FOR INVESTMENT THROUGH CAPITAL CONTRIBUTION, PURCHASE OF SHARES/STAKES BY FOREIGN INVESTORS

1. Foreign investors who make investment through capital contribution or purchase of shares/stakes of business organizations are not required to obtain Investment Certificates.

2. Any business organization invested by a foreign investor through capital contribution or purchase of shares/stakes shall follow procedures for registration of change of members/shareholders at a business registration authority in accordance with regulations of law on enterprises and other regulations of law relevant to its type of business entity.

OPERATION OF INVESTORS EXECUTING INVESTMENT PROJECTS IN INDUSTRIAL PARKS, EXPORT-PROCESSING ZONES, ECONOMIC ZONES, AND HI-TECH ZONES

1. Leasing or purchasing existing buildings, offices, warehouses and depots to serve their business operation.

2. Paying for the use of technical infrastructure and service facilities, including roads, electricity supply, water supply and drainage, communications, treatment of wastes and wastewater, and other public facilities (hereinafter referred to as infrastructure charges)

3. Transferring, receiving the right to use land or lease land with available infrastructure to construct buildings, offices, and other works serving their business operation in accordance with regulations of law on land and real estate trading.

4. Leasing, subleasing their buildings, offices, and other works to serve their business operation in accordance with regulations of law on land and real estate trading.

5. Performing other activities specified in the Law on Investment, and relevant regulations of law.

OPERATION OF INVESTORS EXECUTING INVESTMENT PROJECTS AND OPERATING INFRASTRUCTURE OF INDUSTRIAL PARKS, EXPORT-PROCESSING ZONES, ECONOMIC ZONES, AND HI-TECH ZONES

1. Constructing buildings, offices, warehouses and depots for sale or for lease.

2. Fixing rents for land with available infrastructure; charges for using infrastructure; rents and selling prices for buildings, offices, warehouses and depots, and other services charges as registered with management board. Price brackets and prices for use of infrastructure shall be registered every 6 months or when there are changes.

3. Collecting infrastructure charges.

4. Transfer the right to use land, lease land, sublease land with available infrastructure in industrial parks, export-processing zones, hi-tech zones, economic zones to other investors in accordance with regulations of law on land and real estate trading.

5. Performing other activities specified in the Law on Investment, and relevant regulations of law.

SENDING REPORTS

1. The business organization that executes an investment project shall submit reports only via National Investment Information System.

2. The investment registration authority shall submit physical and electronic reports on National Investment Information System.

RESPONSIBILITIES FOR PROJECT FORMULATION, MAKING INVESTMENT DECISIONS AND EVALUATING INVESTMENTS

1. Investors shall make their own decisions on investment projects; and they shall be responsible for the accuracy and truthfulness of the contents of their registered investment, for their investment project application files and for implementing their investment undertakings as registered.

2. Organizations and individuals authorized to formulate projects, make investment decisions, to evaluate and/or to certify investments shall be liable before the law for their proposals and for their decisions.

SELECTION OF INVESTOR FOR PROJECT WHERE A NUMBER OF INVESTORS SHOW INTEREST

Where two or more investors show interest in an important project identified in master planning for an industry, selection of the investor to implement the project must be conducted by way of tendering in accordance with the laws on tendering.

PREPARATION OF CONSTRUCTION SITES

1. Where land is recovered by the State in accordance with the law on land, the State shall be responsible to recover the land, to pay compensation and to clear the site prior to allocation or lease of the land to the investor.

The recovery of land, payment of compensation and site clearance shall be carried out in accordance with the law on land.

2. Where an investor sub-leases land from a land user to which the State allocates or leases land, the investor shall be responsible to itself arrange payment of compensation and site clearance.

Where the investor has agreed with the land user on the compensation and site clearance but the land user fails to perform the obligations as agreed, the competent people's committee where the investment project is situated shall be responsible for conducting the site clearance prior to hand-over of the site to the investor in accordance with law.

3. In the case of an investment project which complies with the land use zoning approved by the competent State body, the investor shall be permitted to accept an assignment of the land use right or of the lease of the land use right, or to receive capital contribution by way of the land use right from an economic organization, family household or individual in accordance with the law on land without having to carry out procedures for land recovery.

PROCEDURES FOR IMPLEMENTING INVESTMENT PROJECTS INVOLVING MINING AND USE OF NATURAL RESOURCES AND MINERALS

Investment projects involving mining and use of natural resources and minerals shall be implemented in accordance with the law on natural resources and minerals.

IMPLEMENTATION OF INVESTMENT PROJECTS INVOLVING CONSTRUCTION

1. With respect to investment projects involving construction, the formulation, evaluation and approval of the technical design, estimates and total estimated budget shall be carried out in accordance with the law on construction.

2. The investor shall be responsible for the quality of the construction works and for protection of the environment.

Conclusion

Thank you again for downloading this book on *"INVESTMENT: Essential Legal Terms Explained You Need To Know About Law On Investment"* and reading all the way to the end. I'm extremely grateful.

If you know of anyone else who may benefit from the informative legal words presented in this book, please help me inform them of this book. I would greatly appreciate it.

Finally, if you enjoyed this book and feel that it has added value to your study or career in any way, please take a couple of minutes to share your thoughts and post a REVIEW on Amazon. Your feedback will help me to continue to write the kind of Kindle books that helps you get results. Furthermore, if you write a simple REVIEW with positive words for this book on Amazon, you can help hundreds or perhaps thousands of other readers who may want to enhance their legal vocabulary have a chance getting what they need. Like you, they worked hard for every penny they spend on books. With the information and recommendation you provide, they would be more likely to take action right away. We really look forward to reading your review.

Thanks again for your support and good luck!

If you enjoy my book, please write a POSITIVE REVIEW on amazon.

-- *Dr. Peter Johnson* --

Check Out Other Books

Go here to check out other related books that might interest you:

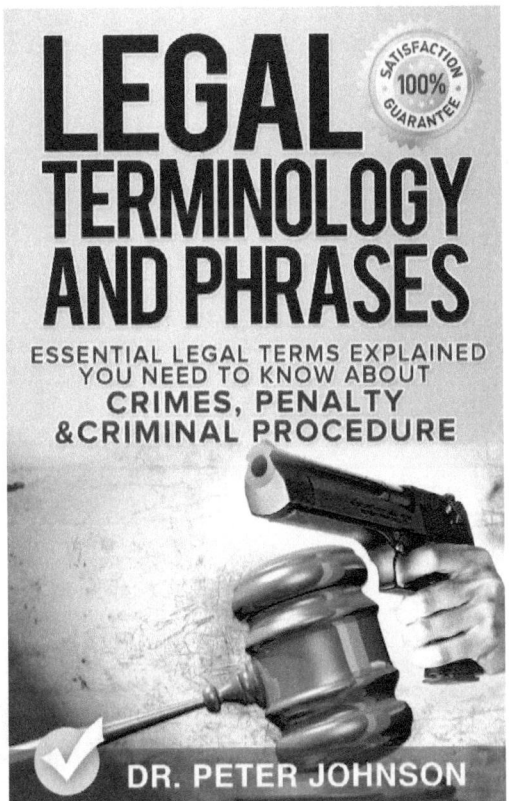

Legal Terminology And Phrases: Essential Legal Terms Explained You Need To Know About Crimes, Penalty And Criminal Procedure

http://www.amazon.com/dp/B01L5EB54Y

COMPANY LAW: Mastering Essential Legal Terms Explained About Limited Liability Companies, Joint-Stock Companies, Partnership, Private Enterprises, And Groups of Companies!

https://www.amazon.com/dp/B07P2PRVMJ

CIVIL LAW: Mastering Essential Legal Terms Explained About Civil Rights, Guardianship, Civil Transactions, Civil Obligations, Civil Liability, Civil Contracts And Civil Procedure!

https://www.amazon.com/dp/B07P5GS8LD

Legal Vocabulary In Use: Master 600+ Essential Legal Terms And Phrases Explained In 10 Minutes A Day

http://www.amazon.com/dp/B01L0FKXPU

Civil Law Vocabulary In Use: Master 350+ Essential Civil Law Terms And Phrases Explained With Examples In 10 Minutes A Day.

https://www.amazon.com/dp/B0781TQWGV

Criminal Law Vocabulary In Use: Master 400+ Essential Criminal Law Terms And Phrases Explained With Examples In 10 Minutes A Day.

https://www.amazon.com/dp/B078KLR51Z

Administrative And Tax Law In Use : Master 300+ Administrative And Tax Law Terms And Phrases Explained With Examples In 10 Minutes A Day.

https://www.amazon.com/dp/B07JMD546J

Productivity Secrets For Students: The Ultimate Guide To Improve Your Mental Concentration, Kill Procrastination, Boost Memory And Maximize Productivity In Study

http://www.amazon.com/dp/B01JS52UT6

Shortcut To Ielts Writing: The Ultimate Guide To Immediately Increase Your Ielts Writing Scores

http://www.amazon.com/dp/B01JV7EQGG

www.ingramcontent.com/pod-product-compliance
Lightning Source LLC
Chambersburg PA
CBHW020606220526
45463CB00006B/2470